GLO

VILLAGE

BURNOUT

Creative Intelligence =

Survival

PHILLIP ROMERO, MD

7.22.2021

Table Of Contents

Preface
Introduction
Preventing Global Burnout
Causes for Global Burnout: The Problem Between Global Brain and Global Mind
Global Mind Vs. Global Burnout
The Human Family vs. Global Burnout
Breaking Free From the Toxic Stress Cycle
#GLOBALMIND PROJECT
Greed and Global Burnout
Detoxing From Global Burnout
The We-Team
Beyond Global Burnout
The Creativity Machine and Global Burnout
Global Mind Against Pandemic
Creativity Versus Pandemic
Dance with Pandemic
COVID Stress: What Is! Vs. What If?
Falling into COVID
Creative Intelligence
Nature's Challenge / Nature's Gift
Redefining Wellness
American Fear Now
About the Author

Preface

GLOBAL VILLAGE BURNOUT: Creative Intelligence = Survival continues exploring biopsychosocial roots of creativity and human cultural evolution that began in *The Art Imperative: The Secret Power of Art* (2010). The research for the Art Imperative started during my Child Psychiatry Fellowship and has been continuous for 35 years. As an artist, I am aware that the roots of my personal creativity are partially genetic and were enhanced during childhood. As a child psychiatrist, I interviewed many artists about how their childhoods shaped their adult artist identity. Among the artists interviewed were Audrey Flack, Louise Bourgeois, Isamu Noguchi, Thomas Downing, Michael Tracy, and I had many informal conversations with Andy Warhol, Martha Graham, and Halston.

Using a biopsychosocial approach to human creativity, I reflect on our present crisis in cultural evolution. Included in this collection of essays are twenty essays published for *ThriveGlobal.com* from 11.2019-6.2021. Over this time-period I had three themes that guided my reflections:

1) The process of Global Village Burnout

2) The cause, COVID Stress + chronic existential stressors from climate change to terrorism

3) The solution to Global Burnout, Creative Intelligence.

The framework for these essays promotes human Creative Intelligence to drive cultural evolution toward *Species Tribalism*. Species Tribalism refers to the shared experience that *homo sapiens* are one biological family whose continued existence requires the evolution of a shared identity. We are not enemies of each other.

We know that human resilience emerges from socially coordinated behavior. In this time of global pandemic, we know that the Global Village must be adequately vaccinated to prevent a chronic pandemic that could mutate, recur, and persist for many years. Only a collective effort to protect the human species can prevent such a catastrophe. Perhaps COVID can trigger our shared Creative Intelligence to mobilize Species Tribalism for survival.

Global Village Stress Contagion: Fear, Anger, Confusion, and Chaos

The COVID pandemic is triggering chronic, toxic global stress. Like the COVID virus, stress in an individual is contagious. Mammals are hardwired to communicate individual stress to the group. From a thumping rabbit to a screaming chimpanzee, to ranting cable news broadcasts, the evolution of social stress communication is designed to preserve the group.

The consequences of socially communicated stress are complex patterns that amplify stressed-out systems. Stress is overwhelming the mind-body of individuals, the social attachments in families, and cultural structures from socioeconomic disparity to racial conflict to religious adversity to political brain-lock. The pre-COVID existential threats of climate change, terrorism, racism, and mass migrations amplify global stress exponentially.

For the individual, the normal stress response to perceived adversity is *freeze-fight-flee.* The feelings of confusion, anger, and fear become conscious almost instantly, and behavior is driven to survive. When the enemy is a chronic existential threat, like climate change or COVID, the brain/mind system feels like a hostage. This triggers a quest for a rescuer. The brain searches for any perceived sanctuary. Individuals in this state may turn to religion, superstition, or sociopathic predators who prey on their fears by offering safety. Self-sabotaging behaviors emerge from chronic stress including over-eating, addiction, workaholism, sex, etc.

For the family, when one member, especially a parent, suffers from toxic stress, the *burnout syndrome* shows up as irritability, isolation, self-sabotaging behaviors, and anxiety. The individual stress of any family member can trigger family-system stress. Like a virus, stress is contagious.

COVID has revealed that mortality is a socioeconomic fact. The rich live longer. The poor die younger. This fresh "X-ray" of the well-known fact of socioeconomic disparity, the "Wealth/Power Pyramid," is activating renewed socio-political activism. Perhaps the new generation can recruit their Creative Intelligence to cultivate meaningful efforts toward the cultural evolution of Species Tribalism. History reveals that acting out destructive revolutions, civil wars, are little more than ineffectual riots and protests that enable the ancient disparity. Greed survives in a new, camouflaged social structure.

What Childhood Reveals: The Infantile Structure of Human Culture

A developmental model frames the chronic stress in civilization as a biopsychosocial phenomenon. Early child development reveals a stage of "parallel play", where children tend not to interact socially during play. The toddler brain has not developed the neural networks for social reciprocity. Among siblings, older sibs can disregard their younger sibs, even harming them to compete for what they want. By the pre-Kindergarten phase, children commence "reciprocal play", and they enjoy the social interaction with their younger siblings and others. Although we teach children The Golden Rule and provide a kindergarten curriculum of "take turns and share," we have not structured civilization adequately with these principles.

Civilization perpetuates the social structures of pre-K sibling rivalry

Insecure attachments kindle neediness and greed during childhood and contribute to narcissistic character patterns in adulthood. These patterns drive bullying during childhood. Although parenting aims to reduce sibling rivalry, human competitiveness is tenacious and can last a lifetime.

The Zero-sum game in the competitive adult world champions self-centered success. With toddler-like attitudes and behaviors, we promote individual dominance and systemic power to attain security.

The Unsustainable Wealth/Power Pyramid

A small minority controls most of the world's wealth and political power. This pyramidal structure reinforces the dominance of the richest.

Like the childhood dynamics of "bully vs. bullied', these patterns perpetually challenge social stability with adversity between the socioeconomic strata. Culture sustains greed as a positive trait. We enable the competitive destructivity, crime, and war in the pyramidal socioeconomic disparity of human civilization. Can we evolve social systems beyond these deep-rooted cultural structures?

The Antidote to Stress: Creative Intelligence

My focus on human creativity as an antidote to chronic stress is grounded with fact-based theories. The crises we face are largely the consequences of human attitudes and behaviors. The human condition is perpetually driven with a struggle to create secure attachments. From the infant-mother attachment to global socioeconomic systems, fear of loss of secure attachments drives human behavior. Conflict, greed, and a need to dominate the competition are hardwired, primordial patterns in individuals and social systems.

We also are endowed with Creative Intelligence, the inborn traits of resilience and creativity that can be cultivated with the human imagination to create solutions for group survival. However, Creative Intelligence must be trained and practiced, like reading or brain surgery.

The great experiment of human species survival depends on Creative Intelligence regulating the inborn self-sabotaging instincts of human destructivity. The ancient mindfulness traditions and modern social neuroscience support the widespread teaching and practice of Creative Intelligence.

A Neo-Renaissance Imperative

One of the most compelling examples of Creative Intelligence is the Renaissance transformation of civilization in the wake of the Great Plague that decimated the world. A small group of wealthy intellectuals with enormous political power, artists, clergy, and writers invented the Renaissance. Supported by the Medici family, this rebirth of the arts would transform the world.

We are facing even more complex challenges as a species now. What happened in Florence must be kindled in the Global Village. Our ancient instincts to band together for group survival always guide us to the creation of new worlds. With the advent of the internet as a Global Brain, the use of Artificial Intelligence, and the socio-emotional motivation to survive, it is imperative to redefine the Global Village. The challenge we face is to nurture the evolution of *Global Mind* capable of empowering self-regulation for the greater good by viewing itself accurately with Species Tribalism.

These essays aim to inspire readers to reinvent themselves as participants in cultural evolution. The Creative Intelligence Imperative activates a bottom-up transformation of individual. Only when we reach a critical mass of mindful brains/minds can we hope to kindle a wave of cultural evolution.

We can take inspiration from the renaissance. Enrico Scrovegni, a prominent banker, promoted Giotto di Bondone to paint the Arena Chapel in Padua. Giotto reinvented painting, activating the viewers with renewed hope and creativity after the devastating plague. One creative idea can trigger a cascade of other creative ideas that can change the world.

Introduction

As a Family psychiatrist, I use the medical evaluation framework, S.O.A.P. (Subjective, Objective, Assessment, Plan), to approach helping stressed-out families mobilize their creative resilience to adversity.

Upscaling this biopsychosocial instrument helps make sense of our stressed-out species in the Global Village. By framing our complex dilemma as the human family overwhelmed with existential threats, teetering on collapse, we can activate our innate Creative Intelligence to develop critical therapeutic interventions.

THE PROBLEM: *A Stressed-out Global Village*

The 7.9 billion human brains on the planet are collectively stressed-out by multiple existential threats. The internet functions like a *Global Brain*, connecting users to the daily event horizon of the stressed-out Global Village. Catastrophic information streams into the viewers brains triggering negative emotions and releasing toxic levels of stress hormones in our body and brain. When the brain is taken hostage by chronic stress hormones, the result is *burnout syndrome.* Anger, fear, confusion, and self-sabotaging attitudes and behaviors hijack the brain/mind, derailing compassion, creativity, and social connectivity. All citizens in the Global Village are vulnerable to these stressors.

Like no other time in history, we are challenged simultaneously with pandemic, climate change (massive fires, colossal storms, melting icecaps and creeping floods), mass migrations, and racial/religious terrorism. All these are consequences of human culture. Global systems, from education to commerce, from religion to medicine, are overwhelmed with stress.

This tidal wave of negative emotional information reveals the extreme socioeconomic disparity where a tiny percentage of the world's population owns most of the wealth and wields enormous power. (https://inequality.org/facts/global-inequality/#global-wealth-inequality). Trust in the structures of civilization is dissolving. The human species is at a tipping point.

THE CAUSE: *Humankind Against Humankind*

The brain substrates of the *mind* reveal multiple centers of consciousness contribute to what we experience as a *self*. We all experience conflicts within ourselves. During protracted periods of stress, the coordination of our thoughts, feelings, memories, and social connectedness breaks down. Self-sabotaging behaviors, interpersonal conflict, and social dysfunction emerge.

Despite 10,000 years of civilization and world-changing technological advances, human relationship patterns remain highly dysfunctional.

Self-sabotaging attitudes and behaviors are rampant. We still cannot accept the most fundamental biological fact: in all our diversity, we are a single species, *homo sapiens.* We have yet to evolve culture that puts this fact into new cultural attitudes and patterns of behavior.

The chronic conflict that threatens us as a species is not the traditional "Human vs. Nature." It is an ancient, greed-driven discourse of "Human vs. Human"—winner take all. A *Global Burnout syndrome* is triggering a collective stress reaction of *freeze-fight-flee* in individual brains and social systems. The result is kindling chaos worldwide.

Tribalism: Natures Challenge

Nature's challenge is rooted in the hardwired survival instincts to survive in tribal groups. The perceived threat from others triggers us to come together and help each other. Group cohesion is the best defense against chronic adversity. Nomadic tribal groups could fight, flee, or live in a chronic state of tribal adversity. As city-states emerged, the option to flee disappeared. In our present-day world, we have become a global village. Chronic adversity between groups spills into the streets, into governing institutions, until systems collapse.

Our competitive drive focuses on overthrowing any perceived threats from other tribes. The zero-sum game of winning and losing, fighting to the death, gave rise to the cultural practices of genocide, slavery, racism, and socioeconomic disparity. Chimpanzees are known to commit genocide of rival groups, despite clear dominance of one group.

Like siblings in a highly dysfunctional family, we murder each other, we steal from each other, we overthrow parental and social structures, and we ultimately self-sabotage our own existence. Despite the kindergarten curriculum of "take turns and share," and the Golden Rule, we have failed as adults to stabilize social connectivity with each other.

THE SOLUTION: *Creative Intelligence*

Nature's gift to humanity is our Creative Intelligence. Creativity is hardwired in the brain and emerges in early childhood. We are also highly resilient, endowed with a complex allostatic system for stress-regulation, individual survival, and complex social mechanisms for group survival. Creativity + Resilience = Creative Intelligence, a trait that can be learned, practiced, and communicated from individuals to groups.

Civilization has evolved from small bands of hunter gatherers whose Creative Intelligence invented painting on cave walls. With art as the springboard for civilization, we have created a Global Village interconnected by a Global Brain—the worldwide web. This Global Brain is at the toddler stage of development—self-centered, greed driven, and undeveloped social mindfulness for self-regulation. There are no adequate "parents" to teach this Brain Mindfulness. Individual groups, like multiple centers of consciousness in the brain, must communicate a shared narrative for self-regulation. We are poised to develop a shared narrative of *Species Tribalism* that redefines us based on biological reality.

THE PLAN: *Toward a Species Tribalism Imperative*

Using a developmental biopsychosocial approach and taking inspiration from how the Medici family kindled the Renaissance, these three points are offered to initiate a discourse for promoting Creativity for group survival.

1. Promote the Species Tribalism Imperative as a *meme*. The idea that *group creativity = group survival* is critical. Individuals, groups, and institutions can use social media, group

education, and corporate policy to advance the new patterns of thinking and cooperation.

2. Promote Mindfulness Training as critical to stress reduction and cultivating a personal experience of compassionate connectivity.

3. Promote Creative Intelligence Training in families. Placing high value on cultivating creative problem-solving during childhood will mitigate the formation of neural pathways in the brain that form insecure attachment and toxic stress. Preventing stress and burnout in adulthood begins in child development. Self-regulation training in childhood is critical to conflict resolution in adulthood. Future generations with a foundation in Creative Intelligence have a greater chance of creating non-adversarial systemic social transformation.

THE PROGNOSIS: *Not with a bang but a whimper*

The patterns of human cultural behavior predict that we may self-terminate the world as we know it. Fear of loss of personal security are escalating with the lack of self-regulation in internet technology. Greed driven patterns of wealth and power acquisition bode for an eventual collapse of the present Global Village structures. As culture overvalues the acquisition of wealth and power, the brain becomes addicted to the pursuit of material attachments. The devaluation of emotional attachment amplifies vulnerability to stress and burnout. A balance of mindfulness contemplation and healthy competition promote longevity and wellness.

With the vanishing of a Third-world, low-cost labor force, the 10,000-year-old 'master-slave' socioeconomic architecture, which produced our present-day world, cannot bear the emerging stress load. With 50.8% of the world's population plugged into the internet, the impoverished masses are empowered to disrupt the socioeconomic pyramid.

Human creativity, almost fully monopolized by the wealthiest socioeconomic strata, must face a self-reckoning. Will this minority take inspiration from the Medici's and lead us toward Species Tribalism? Or will it cling to its own greed-driven social structures and make war on the masses. History tells us that war is the usual pattern of behavior.

It is up to us to focus our Creative Intelligence and reframe our lives as members of a single family.

PART I
GLOBAL BURNOUT

Chapter 1
Preventing Global Burnout

From Global Brain to Global Mind This mindset shift will help you deal with stress.

There's no doubt about it: we are experiencing global human family stress. In today's internet-addicted culture, we are triggered emotionally by an information tsunami overwhelming our minds and bodies.

Brain/screen interfacing has amplified. We are beginning to understand the negative consequences of screen usage and screen addiction. Families are experiencing routine stresses correlated with how screens isolate individuals from personally connecting to other another, resulting in burnout, teen screen addiction, anxiety, depression, and even suicide.

From family burnout to global burnout

From Facebook to Fake News, we are inundated by a continuous flow of negative opinionizing and bullying that triggers stress. We already know that when our stress response is continuously activated, it becomes physiologically toxic. And toxic stress triggers anger, fear, and confusion, hijacking our calm, connected, creative natures.

The challenge to regulate the internet's toxicity and promote more interpersonal connection will require the participation of individuals, Organizations, and content-creation platforms to generate what I call Global Mind.

What is Global Mind?

The problems we see in our "global village" is a macro version of the chronically stressed-out relationships that occur in nuclear family systems.

In my 30 years—approximately 40,000 hours—of direct patient care in my adult, child, and family psychiatry practice, I have trained thousands of individuals, couples, families, and family businesses in stress regulation. I have seen firsthand that toxic stress in family systems—the me-against-you script—can be unlearned. Training the family in what I call a "We" narrative—the We Team or *MYWe* (Me + You = We), for short—reframes the individual reality to a shared group reality.

When an individual feels more secure attachment in their family, negative stress is transformed into excitement or neutralized for empathetic connection. Creativity is amplified and shared attention strengthens emotional bonds. It's "all for one and one for all"—the traditional mantra of tribal identity.

That is why I believe our global village can and must unlearn the script that keeps us in a state of isolation and toxic stress. This is where the Global Mind steps in. At its core, it is the self-regulatory instincts of human beings. The Global

Mind concept sees the internet as a Global Brain—driven by self-serving emotions with little self-regulation.

Given how we use and depend on the internet today, we have yet to see the emergence of a true Global Mind. And though the internet has intensified feelings of stress and disconnection, it also presents a distinct opportunity to translate and apply effective clinical principles for family stress regulation training to the global family system.

Moving toward species tribalism

If we think of the internet as an extension of the brain, then content platforms are like the brain's modules of consciousness. Our brain has two structures that generate two narratives: the emotional brain and the mindful brain.

The emotional brain is ancient and focused on our survival, whereas the mindful brain is involved in abstract thinking, creativity, language, and mindful reflection. We know that the mindful brain (cortex) can regulate the emotional brain (limbic system). This self-regulatory ability is critical to generating social connectivity, conflict resolution, cultural creativity, and resilience. When brain/mind consciousness coordinates with social behavior, our creative nature thrives.

The human brain/mind therefore provides a model of mindful self-regulation that can be made accessible to anyone through technology, such as apps to encourage the emergence of Global Mind. This carries the potential to find solutions to the myriad threats to our species and our planet, preventing Global Burnout.

The encouraging news in this time of divisiveness and mindless conflict is the rise of many mindful narrators like thought leaders, moral and ethical leaders, ecosystem advocates, and identity validators. The obstacles we face now require us to integrate, coordinate, and validate these mindful groups into a narrative not just for cultural tribalism but for *species* tribalism, thereby linking millions of mindful cultural narratives to fulfill our evolutionary potential. It is possible for our internet to generate a synchronized stream of positive, creative, awareness and give rise to more unity with one another.

Onward!

My aim in this series is to introduce the Global Mind concept as a cultural evolutionary process. Creating, experimenting, and practicing ways to generate this sense of "MYWe" over the internet is the one of the most significant investments we can make in one another. It will require emotionally intelligent technologies to become more commonplace.

In this series, I will explore:

- The evolving Global Mind concept
- Why Global Burnout may be inevitable

- My clinical work in brain/mind training with stressed out families
- The four core problems of global relationship stress
- How we can promote the emergence of species tribalism.
- — Published on November 14, 2019

Chapter 2

Causes for Global Burnout: The Problem Between Global Brain and Global Mind

Brain-Screen Stress

S. O. A. P. defines the heart of medical practice. Physicians are trained to evaluate their patient's state of health by looking at the *Subjective* story of the problem, an *Objective* examination, an *Assessment* (reconciling a patient's story with what is happening with their body), and the *Plan* or recommended course of action. This empathic alliance with the patient ensures a cooperative "we team" to facilitate treatment and optimize recovery.

To better understand today's challenges, think of our global village as a patient. We can then use the S.O.A.P framework for insight.

One culprit behind why the world is in a perpetual state of chaos and suffering is the internet, our newly evolved, emotionally driven Global Brain. It is worthwhile to think of the internet as an electronic nervous system and global emotional brain. Screens reach over half of the world's population—that is an astounding 3.2 billion human brains. Because of a constant content stream, we are habitually and inadvertently generating toxic stress. Sooner or later, all stressed-out systems fall apart, which makes us susceptible to global burnout.

The Attachment Problem

Buddha was right when he said life is suffering: our subjective experience of suffering begins before we are born and follows us to our final breath. The objective truth is that our bodies cling to life. Attachment, as Buddha says, gives rise to the visceral fear of the loss of attachment. As mammals, secure attachments are critical for our survival: physical, mental, emotional, and social.

We struggle to make sense of our existence through awareness and language, the primary ingredient to forming culture. Meaningful narratives generate cultures—religion, customs, and family values—that bind people together to belief systems that promote resilience and survival. However, our experience of reality is relative to our individual point of view. The truth is that there is no universal truth.

Each of us grows up as an individual connected to a family system and in any family system there is a natural conflict between the system and the self. But what adds to the challenge now is that children's developing brains are plugged into the internet from their earliest years as part of their attachment. Screens often command more attention and loyalty than parents, distorting individual perception and family dynamics.

I recently saw a family of three at the airport: Mom and Dad were completely absorbed with their phone screens, and their two-year-old sat on the floor with his tablet. Each person was relating to their screen and not to each other. The child's brain is forming an attachment to the screen as his security blanket, displacing his need for a living companion. His memories at this age may not be retrievable in adulthood, but they will shape his emotional security.

The tools we create change us, the users. We can use our tools creatively or destructively. How will we regulate our use of everyday technology? We have no idea how we will evolve.

The Brain/Mind Problem

If you walk into your dark apartment, exhausted after a long day, and you perceive an intruder, you will jump. Your emotional brain activates the fight-flight-freeze response. When you fumble to turn on the light and see nobody is there, you relax. What just happened?

Neuroscientist Michael Gazzaniga theorizes that the brain generates many minds, or modules of consciousness, through different cortical neural networks—the brain's outer thinking layer—when they are supported by the inner emotional brain's processing. We experience a flow of consciousness because the brain orchestrates communication between these different modules and develops a single narrative. This is the emotional foundation of our sense of self.

So, when you walk into your dark apartment, your emotional brain, already full of the day's stress hormones, perceives a threatening form and jumps away from an intruder. When the higher order thinking brain takes over, it flips on that proverbial light: behold, there is no danger.

Screens offer—and can skew—perception. Like the instant emotional response to the perceived intruder in the example above, the internet can trigger an instinctive, mindless response. It is necessary to "turn on the lights" of our mind to successfully navigate internet content. Without mindful self-regulation, screen use can become addictive and self-sabotaging.

The Two Brain-Script Problem

Our brain creates two narrative streams: the emotional body story and the thoughtful mind story. However, what you *feel* and what you *think* often come into conflict.

The emotional brain is impulsive, unconscious, and powerful. This ancient structure lives in what I call the limbic script or the 5 Fs: freeze, fight, and flee when danger is perceived, and when we feel safe, we feed and fornicate to nourish the body and reproduce.

Contrast that with our mindful script—abstract thinking, creativity, curiosity, and mindful reflection. It is because of the mindful brain that we are capable of learning and transforming our sense of self.

The miracle of neuroplasticity, the brain's ability to change, gives great hope that millions of people can learn to change attitudes and behaviors. Individual mindful evolution can connect us to each other.

By rerouting the adrenaline-driven negative emotions that elicit acting out in anger, fear, and confusion, mindful awareness activates problem solving, excitement stress, and conjoint creativity.

We can then be more instinctively calm, seeking connection, and ready to creatively solve meaningful problems together, whether it is in childhood play or the challenge of global climate change. An individual mind is ready to participate in creating a new, mindful social system: from Me to You to what I call "MYWe."

The Brain-Screen Stress Problem

In today's screen culture, we are vulnerable to overwhelming non-conscious emotions triggered by the internet's constant information tsunami. When our brains are constantly consuming screen content, our stress triggers become chronic, our brains are hijacked by stress hormones, and we become addicted to screens and live as hostages of our negative emotions.

An example of what screens have done to us is Facebook Addiction Disorder (FAD). People with depression who use Facebook as a coping mechanism are at an increased risk for developing FAD, which may reinforce depression symptoms, according to findings by Julia Brailovskaia, PhD, at Ruhr-Universität Bochum, Germany. Published in Cyberpsychology, Behavior, and Social Networking, she said, "We need more cross-cultural, longitudinal, experimental research to understand the development and maintenance of Facebook Addiction Disorder.

Ramesh Srinivasan, UCLA Professor and Director of the UC Digital Cultures Lab, expressed his concern about the internet, writing, "It can create a world where we are all placed in bubbles, where the systems themselves can be manipulated by people who don't have our best interests in mind."

When screen content is emotionally negative, our emotional brain disconnects from our mindful brain. Our fight-flight-freeze response is activated and it's easy for us to turn against each other. Our biases are amplified. We build resentments. We feel self-pity. We blame others and ourselves. We have panic attacks, anxiety, and depression. We struggle for control. And the struggle is endless; we can never seem to get control of what we believe will give us security. We burn out.

Toward Burnout Prevention

The fact that we are now a neurologically linked species reframes our sense of self. We are no longer alone. We have a choice—to plug in or not to plug in. Embracing this cultural evolution mindfully offers hope that the rudimentary Global Brain may generate a Global Mind capable of caring for, protecting, and nourishing one another and our planet. The choice is ours, individually and collectively.

— Published on November 28, 2019

Chapter 3

Global Mind Vs. Global Burnout

How we can kindle he emergence of Global Mind

Your kids are screaming, making noise, and attacking each other. You are screaming back at them and feel no support from your co-parent. As a parent, when your emotional brain is disconnected from its creative, mindful brain, you may feel like saying, "Get me out-a here!"

Contrast this to when you feel supported by your co-parent. When your calm co-parent is present and empathetic to all, the family system calms down. Everyone refocuses on the new parental narrative that invites reconnection with one another.

What has happened is that the calm co-parent's emotional brain can think, activate creative problem-solving, and find ways to resolve distressed family signals? In other words, cool cognition regulates hot emotion.

Can we generate an instinctive, calm Global Mind across the internet—a digital version of that calm co-parent? This challenge presents the most complex obstacle to human cultural evolution.

From the nuclear family to the global village

Secure attachment to our body begins in infancy. The foundation of a true self is laid down in the brain's circuits, when a mother gazes into her baby's eyes and the baby mirrors her gaze back. Trust in the care-giving environment and family shapes our creative resilience.

When families provide "good enough" love, empathy, and validation, a child's natural wonder is kindled, urging them to explore the world and create new attachments. This is the beginning of social mind.

These new attachments inform a child's sense of connection and tribal belonging, as well as provide a shared family narrative. In his book *The Consciousness Instinct: Unraveling the Mystery of How the Brain Makes the Mind*, Michael Gazzaniga describes how the brain's multiple modules of consciousness create a singular narrative of emotion and cognition that form a sense of self. A child's sense of self emerges as the brain matures, becoming part of the family identity.

Similarly, if the global village is analyzed under the purview of the individual brain/mind and family dynamics, the internet can play a role in nurturing that sense of security and trust in one another. The Global Mind Concept envisions an internet with myriad modules of consciousness—social, science, art, economics, religion—communicating in a coherent, humanistic narrative of compassion, connectivity, and creativity.

To continue thriving, the global village needs a stronger sense of species tribalism, a coherent experience of identification with others. When seven billion brains instantaneously connect over the internet, mirroring each other, the primary response is emotional, both positive and negative. It will take an ambitious, coordinated effort to activate the potential for generating a reflective Global Mind to produce species tribalism.

How can this be done?

Our Global Mind

Our greatest challenge to species survival is kindling a Global Mind with instinctive care and compassion. Like the individual brain/mind, where self-awareness confers a visceral connection to the body, Global Mind has the potential for connecting billions of human bodies with a shared sense of being and purpose. Global Mind offers the greatest hope to collectively regulate the immense diversity across our planet and tip us away from the natural biases and competitive distrust we have of others. Instead, we move toward connection.

Just half of the 7.5 billion brain/minds on the planet are connected by the internet. We are still so divisive among our fellow human beings that it is hard to imagine a gradual emergence of a Global Mind without an intensive, concerted effort, such as a Global Mind Project, much like the Space Project of the 1960s.

A Global Mind Project

Fortunately, we are witnessing a worldwide cry streaming across the internet for freedom, autonomy, and respect. Unfortunately, it is motivated by escalating political oppression, climate change, and failing pre-internet systems (monetary systems, trade systems, economic inequity).

Countless humanistic movements show up across the internet, from mindful meditation to "save the environment" to self-empowerment groups. But a coherent narrative has yet to emerge that will have a palpable self-regulating effect on the global system.

A *Global Mind Project* will require a truly consilient effort. In <u>Consilience: The Unity of Knowledge</u>, evolutionary biologist E.O. Wilson talks about consilience as the unification of different knowledge domains. The fact is that we are generating new platforms of knowledge—from biology to artificial intelligence to the emotional fabric of relationships—to create a shared narrative on the internet. However, fear-based stories persist, halting progress. So-called "World War Zero" is an example of a consilient effort to address climate change as an existential threat to the planet. Like so many movements, it comes and goes as a topic of interest and action.

If we are to generate a coherent experience of shared mindful self-regulation using the internet, it will take an extraordinary effort that looks beyond a singular problem to figuring out how to produce a Global Mind Project with meaningful results. This can only happen when global burnout becomes a more obvious and acknowledged threat to our lives.
— Published on December 11, 2019

Chapter 4

The Human Family vs. Global Burnout

The phrase, *"Global Burnout,"* was tattooed into my emotional memory on September 11, 2001. I called my daughter at SUNY Stoney Brook to share the news, "The World has changed. It will never be the same." We wept together. The human family system had cracked. What was happening in my lifetime?

When studying the art of children who witnessed the 9/11 tragedy, I realized that the clinical lessons from treating traumatized children and families could be translated into a narrative intervention for our stressed-out global village in the face of numerous modern triggers and traumas.

And the most accessible medium for this intervention is the internet.

Because our brains are constantly connecting through an interactive screen, linking billions of fellow human beings could boost mindful cultural evolution… or be a rabbit hole for cultural devolution. Can we muster the emotional intelligence, the political will, and the cultural resilience to adopt a positive outlook for the emergence of a healing, humanistic global narrative — what I now call "Global Mind"?

Empowering a "We-team"

With each new generation comes the birth of possible changes for the human family. Culture begins in the family. Parents wield enormous power to change the attitudes and behaviors from their generation that are passed onto their children. Traditions are taught that promote resilience and connectivity — after all, open-minded parents produce open-minded children. But old biases are also passed on and these can perpetuate toxic stress.

In working with stressed-out families, it is critical to help parents activate their creative powers in what I call the "we-team." Parents have the power to create a coherent family narrative that binds members together — trust in the family is the most powerful human narrative for species survival.

The bio-psycho-social fabric of the self is emotionally enmeshed with the family mind, where parents regulate, train, and coach their children into a "we" narrative. The everyday stresses of family attachment trigger disconnection that require reconnection. For instance, the push-back between toddlers and parents — between "me" and "you" — begins at the first utterance of "no" and becomes an existential conflict at puberty, when the brain's abstract capabilities emerge. Such developmental milestones form the basis of a secure sense of self when so-called "good enough" parenting guides a child toward reconnection with validation and empathy.

Phantom stress

The brain has two narrative structures: the body brain (the emotional brain or limbic system), and the mindful, storytelling brain (prefrontal cortex). A stressed-out limbic system disconnects from the mindful brain, just as stressed-out family members withdraw from one other.

We know that trauma in early development has a profound effect on brain development, particularly the amygdala. Elevated stress hormones cause the amygdala to grow, becoming more sensitive and easily triggered later in life. A family that validates a child's trauma, empathizes with confusion, and soothes fear and helplessness will provide security against toxic stress and curb amygdala hypertrophy.

I teach my patients to be aware of the distinction between the limbic narrative — *freeze-fight-flight* — and the mindful script — *calm-connected-creative*. The mindful brain can reframe the body's stressed-out state through calm breathing. Within minutes, a calm mind adapts to whatever stress the family is in, rather than feed reactive anger, fear, and confusion. Calm minds cool hot-tempered bodies.

My eyes were opened to the power of calm consciousness after spending a summer in Dharmsala, India, during medical school, studying Tibetan medicine, meditation, and philosophy. I met the Dalai Lama, had extensive mindfulness training, and was steeped in Buddhist studies. One of the most impactful lessons of my life and career at that time is that everything is connected.

By integrating developmental neuroscience, mindfulness practice, and Buddha's Four Noble Truths, I found parents eager to learn about how mindful awareness helps them regulate stress. When a co-parenting team learns to detoxify negative emotions that hijack their brains and destroys their loving bonds, they can share a deep sense of family security. In other words, training parents with mindful stress-regulation skills produces secure family connections for individuals, couples, and families.

A Viral Global Mind Narrative

The greatest stories ever told to shape human behavior and forge connection are the Bible — 2.4 billion followers and a 2,000-year run, and the Koran with 1.9 billion followers. In *Narrative Economics: How Stories Go Viral and Drive Major Economic Events*, Nobel Laureate Robert Shiller explains how human economic behaviors are activated by emotionally charged stories of idealistic and catastrophic investment possibilities. This is true beyond the realm of economics.

Our need for a shared narrative is becoming more evident throughout our global village. Such a narrative could promote more trust and help us be less self-centered to create a global "we team." On the internet and in life, the current story we share is driven by our base emotions, both positive and negative. We need a new narrative of shared meaning and system regulation that helps us to avoid the conflict and violence marking so much of our history and current events.

Technology is a boon, and we need to learn how to harness it for shared mindfulness — or Global Mind — and combat shared toxic stress. A viral Global Mind narrative must inspire longevity, shape behaviors at all levels of communication, and awaken us to the obvious: human beings are one family and share one story — that of bio-psycho-social survival.

But can we consolidate enough humanistic narratives to promote a cultural evolutionary leap towards *species tribalism*?

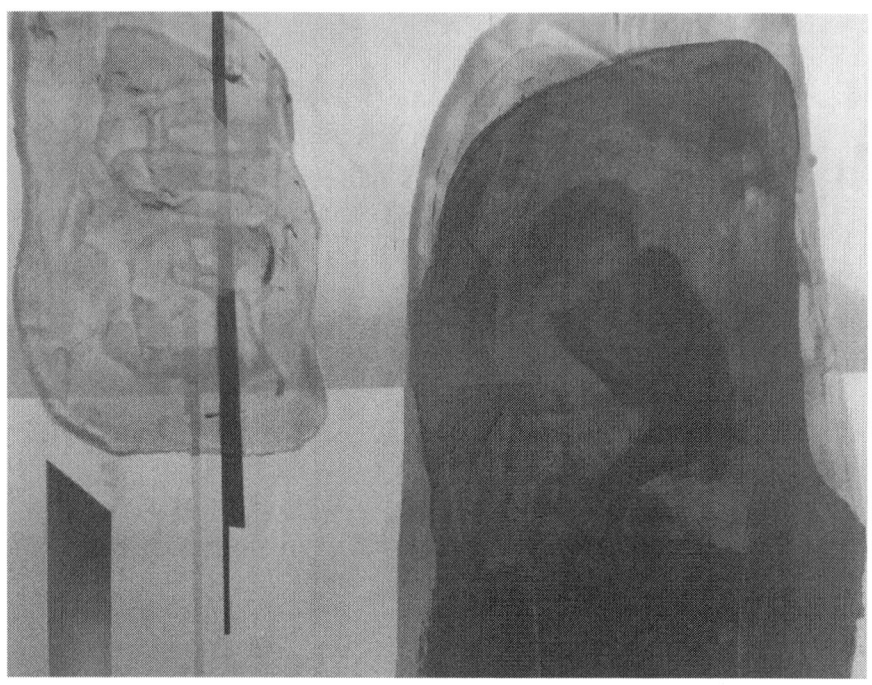

ARTIFICIAL ANNUNCIATION 1975 PHILLIP ROMERO
— Published on December 29, 2019

Chapter 5
Breaking Free From the Toxic Stress Cycle

I developed *Logosoma Brain Training (LBT)* in 1986 to train individuals, couples, and families for relationship stress regulation and to create a secure "We-team" narrative. LBT focuses on three goals for attentional training.

First is just to relax, to recover from the daily stress triggers. This can be accomplished by a simple, repetitive focus on breathing or counting, also called "the relaxation response."

Second is to focus on two questions to distinguish your false self from your true self: What am I afraid of? What are my wishes?

Third is to cultivate a sense of deeper personal meaning by focusing on benevolent concepts like compassion, forgiveness, acceptance, gratitude, connectedness, and impermanence.

Mindful awareness is not a "mystical" exercise. You do not have to sit in a lotus position, but you might want to consider using a scented candle to enhance your memory and relaxation. Mindful awareness is an introspective and repetitive practice. Mindful awareness focuses your conscious attention inward, toward the flow of your own mental and emotional processes. By learning to observe your own thoughts like an independent spectator, you will begin to gain a sharpened awareness of exactly what you are thinking and feeling. Mindful awareness is critical to Logosoma Brain Training, to the building of new attitudes, habits, and language that will retrain your brain and reshape your connections with others.

The logosoma practice of mindful awareness is based on ancient meditation techniques from the Far East and the exciting new discovery of *neuroplasticity,* the brain's built-in ability to rewire itself and form new neuronal connections. In recent years, neuroscientists have proven your brain is not fixed but can be remodeled. Through focused attention over time, you can rewire your brain's synaptic connections.

Neuroplasticity makes it possible for you to break old destructive habits by rewiring your brain to develop a new resilient sense of authenticity in your identity, longer lasting love with your mate, and emotionally secure bonds with your family and social network. This is exactly how emotional healing in psychotherapy works. By retelling your story, by remembering old wounds, by reflecting on patterns of self-sabotaging behaviors and by initiating new life patterns based on your wishes, you begin to rewire your brain to become your true self.

Excerpt from *Phantom Stress: Brain Training To Master Relationship Stress* by Phillip E. Romero

M.D., with permission from the author and publisher.

— Published on January 2, 2020

Chapter 6
#GLOBALMIND PROJECT

A Meme for 2020

The cultural advances that created the post-World War global village are falling apart. World systems are in gridlock and political factions are in brain-lock. Contagious narratives of blame and self-pity run amok on the streets and the internet. Our world is convulsing with conflict and outrage.

Why is this happening? Once an individual brain is hijacked by toxic stress, it becomes hostage to hate, fear, and confusion. The stressed-out brain then triggers self-sabotaging, compulsive behaviors. The most recent example is the US-Iran swapping military strikes that could trigger world conflict. If our global village succumbs to these base urges, and a viral narrative of hate and fear hijacks millions of brains, our survival is in peril.

The Internet is a Child

The internet functions as a global emotional brain, much like a child's brain. The child brain rapidly develops in the prepubescent years to operate its body, socialize, and begin learning about the world. Families and cultures start teaching self-regulation to children by the age of two. Parental guidance provides the child's brain with a top-down message to learn behavioral norms and cultivate attitudes for socialization. That's how toddlers learn to engage with their peers—rather than just play side-by-side—which is much more fun, but also charged with potential conflict.

At puberty, a great leap in cognitive development occurs, activating abstract thinking and the capacity for mindful reflection. Tweens can now scare themselves with existential anxiety. Between puberty and 25 years of age, brain growth explodes and goes through a period of pruning whereby neural networks that are cultivated through practice survive for life.

Cultivating a Mindful Internet

Because children's brains are sponges, it is important to acknowledge how the internet is affecting development. For a child, the internet is everywhere: practically on any device with a screen at home and in the classroom. They are being hijacked by the internet.

That is why mindfulness training is best started at a young age. By practicing self-regulation and emotional communication, parents can apply similar principles to teach children how to use the internet mindfully. The internet needs the equivalent of parental guidance, but its owners and designers have yet to develop and apply a parenting perspective in their mission and invention.

The internet needs a universal code of conduct that helps users keep ethics, morals, and self-regulation front-of-mind. Can we activate a culture that creates a mindful internet—a more ethical, compassionate, mindful machine?

The Global Mind Meme

Global Mind is a narrative, hypothesis, and potential cultural *meme.* Like the neural messages from the mindful brain (pre-frontal cortex) to the emotional brain (limbic system), Global Mind memes can serve as self-awareness reminders, redirecting the internet's self-centered, impulsive urges toward greater reflective participation.

Habituating to mindful awareness every time you "plug in" is a potential influence on culture. For example, imagine you are watching a YouTube video of a piano-playing kitten. As you watch, you take a moment to reflect on what it reminds you of, such as the memory of a moving concert. You can now reframe that kitten video with a shared comment compassionate connection, such as, "The kitten reminds me of how connected I felt to others at this inspiring concert years ago."

As we experience deeper self-awareness, our natural connections and innate compassion are enhanced. Promoting this calm connectivity can be shared around the world with a Global Mind meme project.

Mission Possible?

To realize a Global Mind requires a viral awakening far beyond the education and awareness offered by present-day social movements. Such a leap forward needs to integrate multiple narratives across the internet and consistently reiterate our shared stories. The idea is to recruit the individual reflections of users, platform hosts, and algorithm designers to remind us that we are members of a whole, the global village.

Global Citizen is a good example of what can be done when a concept activates individuals from the bottom-up. However, the celebrity status of such projects can be like the July Fourth fireworks: impressive and glittery, but with limited on-the-ground change in behaviors and attitudes.

Since we are constantly being fed memes, why not share Global Mind memes that become a habit *and* a way of thinking, feeling, and doing? These shared images have the potential to make Global Mind a way of *being*.

Creative Kindling

To encourage greater introspection and optimism, we must regulate our indulgences in a jaded world of skeptics, ambivalent bystanders, and glamorized over-consumption. Cataclysmic fantasies come easy and are profitable, but that does not really help anybody. We love to scare ourselves, but we need to generate enough concern about each other to practice a new way of being human.

If we acknowledge and accept the impact of our competitive natures, self-centered drives, and predisposition to lie and cheat, we can use the internet to mindfully regulate a new story of fellowship and family.

Generating and augmenting our natural empathy with Global Mind memes is just one way to accomplish this.

A Wave of New Storytellers

The potential for Global Mind memes is already clear and present. We are witnessing a rapid emergence of thought leaders contributing their personal experiences, research, and observations that can be applied to assuage global burnout. Many authors have called for social and environmental mindfulness—book titles from the last three years alone sound like a chorus of Global Mind memes!

- *Behave: The Biology of Humans at Our Best and Worst* by Robert Sapolsky
- *Don't Be Evil: How Big Tech Betrayed Its Founding Principles—and All of Us* by Rana Foroohar
- *Minds Make Societies: How Cognition Explains the World Humans Create* by Pascal Boyer.

Then there are the next generation of activist-storytellers, like *Time*'s Person of the Year, Greta Thunberg, who demands awareness, accountability, and action to beat the global climate change challenge.

Another example is the *Brilliant Minds* podcast, which was launched in 2015. It became the basis of the *Brilliant Minds Foundation*, which aims to promote "Swedish values," such as openness, transparency, equality, trust, and social responsibility. The foundation sponsors new discourse in global self-awareness through conversations between diverse thought leaders. Conversations are crucial, as we see in family life, since they continue to shape behavior and advance mindful culture.

Triggering #GlobalMind

Global Mind is springing up spontaneously. Deeply felt, scientifically grounded, creative narratives are emerging. If we take them as a signal that the cultural evolution of global self-regulation is being born, perhaps a Global Mind meme project can empower a new organizational hierarchy where the power, profit, and control that shape internet culture can encourage more mindful interaction within the different communities we are members of.

— Published on January 8, 2020

Chapter 7
Greed and Global Burnout

When Resources Run Out in the Global Garden
"Greed is good."
"Too much ain't enough."
"Greed is the root of all evil."

These are just a few examples of our society's polarized attitude towards greed. The human brain is genetically wired for greed, which can become compulsive and addictive, altering our ability to deal with the painful realities of life.

And any addiction can lead to individual, family, or communal burnout. When chronic, toxic stress hijacks human systems, from the nuclear family to the global village, greed drives massive self-sabotaging behaviors, such as the overuse and abuse of natural resources.

When resources dry up in our global village, socio-cultural debates and political conflicts will be meaningless. However, what is meaningful right now is recovery from compulsive, self-destructive patterns. Such recovery requires changes in our attitudes and behaviors, including (1) acceptance of our limitations to change others; and (2) gratitude for our ability to rewire our brains, thereby creating new circuits for self-regulation.

Accepting that our planet has limited resources requires us to become mindful caretakers to sustain the "global garden" that is our home. Can we awaken a so-called gardener-mind to regulate greed and our more damaging impulses?

Masters of the Universe

The human conflict between creativity and greed continuously reverberates from our genetic structure to our world's cultural systems. Promoter genes in DNA activate replication and resilience to life's stressors. We know that secure parent-infant bonds stimulate promoter genes, making it clear that positive emotional connection literally keeps our species alive.

Despite the strength of the positive emotional connection, this is tested when different values contradict what our promoter genes have prepared us for. A good place to see this play out is in the running of financial markets. Financial markets are largely overseen by men seeking to attain "master of the universe" status—they are driven by ever-perpetuating greed.

Science reveals that testosterone and dopamine drive the hunt for profit, just as they drove our ancestors to pursue animals for food. In the life of a Wall Street trader, for example, high morning testosterone levels drive confidence and winning trades spikes testosterone levels. This triggers grandiosity and increases risky behavior. The emotional high impairs judgment and drives greed at any cost.

Patrick Messel from Freie Universität Berlin says, "Greed predicts selfish economic decisions... at the expense of others. This effect was amplified when individuals strived for obtaining real money, as compared to points, and when their revenue was at the expense of another person, as compared to a computer."

The Science

Brain studies distinguish two centers at play in financial evaluation: the nucleus accumbens and the anterior insula. The nucleus accumbens is activated by high risk-taking traders when they "go for the kill." This causes a surge in nature's feel-good chemical, dopamine, which reinforces risk-taking behavior.

On the other hand, risk-averse investors activate the *anterior insula, the brain center* that responds to a rancid smell or a coiled snake. The resulting 'freeze' response can paralyze mindful reflection and careful risk analysis, leading to missed opportunities.

Neuroeconomist, Paul Zak studies how oxytocin, the "calm and connect" hormone and neurotransmitter, affects moral attitudes and behavior. "People who are greedy have brains that work differently…their character traits are similar to those of psychopaths…and the dysfunctional processing of oxytocin in their brains appears to be one reason for this."

Women produce much higher levels of oxytocin than men, predisposing them to be potentially better decision-makers for the group. With the current surge in active female empowerment movements like Time's Up and #MeToo, we may see significant cultural shifts—including attitudes towards greed—with more widespread women's leadership in government and business.

The Global Mind Project

The internet models as a global emotional brain and invites the imagination to explore possible ways to promote sustainable cultural evolution. This can help us move past greed, as well as be more mindful of our resources and for each other. Designing such an ambitious *Global Mind Project* (GMP) will require a sustained effort with many layers of socio-cultural collaboration. Before it can be implemented, though, the essential ingredients need to be linked.

The GMP requires a coordinated integration of neuroscience, artificial intelligence (AI), and social media. Translational social neuroscience and evolutionary biology can offer a scientific foundation. AI is needed to address technological complexity. And social media must deliver a unifying story of purpose to ignite urgency throughout our global village.

When the built-in creativity of the brain drives social connectivity into a "we-team" narrative, we will become more capable of solving the most challenging problems that threaten our survival.

— Published on January 27, 2020

Chapter 8
Detoxing From Global Burnout

Creative Resilience from Chronic Stress and Anger

To commemorate Holocaust Memorial Day, world leaders gathered in remembrance and global mindfulness. This exercise is not just a show of respect and solidarity for all the victims of World War II, but more critically, it is a demonstration of how mindfulness can positively affect our chronic, historic stress and our sense of community.

Remembering the Damage Done

After World War I, traumatized Germany was seduced into a mindless narrative of paranoia, scapegoating, and rage to mobilize tribal warfare. The collective shame, the physical catastrophe, and the economic disparity over losing the Great War provoked a second World War driven by mindless revenge. The stressed-out post-war culture was led to a self-sabotaging end.

The brain sees the world as a zero-sum game: survive or perish. When survival hormones hijack the stressed-out brain, it becomes extremely difficult to keep our mindful, self-regulating identity. Normalizing a narrative of fear, anger, and confusion alters the brain's perception of what is safe versus what is dangerous, resulting in our self-perception as victims. The "us against them" story feels correct, and blaming others continues this narrative. We become hostages of a perpetual victim script.

Survival at any cost is hardwired, so it becomes easy to rationalize and minimize any destructive behaviors that promote "winning." When groups, tribes, and cultures bond with this emotional distortion of reality, we see collective denial, racism, subjugation, and dehumanization.

The two World Wars are extreme examples of what chronic stress and global burnout can do to us. And it's important to remember that the biological possibility of cultural burnout is present with every new generation of human beings. Stressed-out brains become self-sabotaging. When cultures cascade into collective burnout, driven by present-day stressors and amplified by phantom stressors from the past, we can literally relapse into a cycle of addictive, self-destructive behavior.

The Tipping Point

We are at a cultural tipping point that is actively triggering global stress. We stress over contamination of our ecosystem, gender bias, economic disparity, unregulated cyber security, nuclear holocaust, nationalism, religious Armageddon…and the list goes on. There is even a *Doomsday Clock.*

Since prehistoric times, we see our world as eternally renewable. Our sense of entitlement has made us oblivious to the role we have played as architects of clear and present stressors. In the name of tribal, national, or international security, we have allowed greed—for money, power, and resources—to fuel the very conflicts that incite our fear, anger, confusion.

In the last century, it is the potential for nuclear war that awakened us to a simple fact: nothing lasts forever, including Mother Earth's finite resources. Our greed and mindless acceptance of "us versus them" will destroy our planet and ourselves.

But we can choose differently. We can choose to change ourselves, our attitudes, and behaviors so that we are more mindful and take better care of the Earth and our communities. We can choose humility and empathy so that we live in thriving societies that support all of us, rather than just a chosen, wealthy few. We can choose to monitor ourselves with an eye toward managing our resources responsibly and sustainably.

The existential threats that we all face sparks the need for *species tribalism,* or a coherent experience of identification with others. Acceptance of our shared biology, genes, and emotional need for security shall pave the way toward a shared narrative of survival and sustainability. The time to put dreams and hopes and possibilities into action is *now.*

The New Priority

Once the individual brain is in burnout and the self-sabotaging circuits are on, anger, fear, and confusion dominate behavior. Anger in action awakens the beast within. When voices in leadership validate and direct this anger toward destructive behavior, the perpetual victim script is activated, and chaos ensues.

To challenge the emergence of angry, power-hungry leadership around the world, a bottom-up stream of Global Mind—more widespread, mindful self-regulation—can create new narratives of cooperation and creative problem-solving. We cannot expect our present leaders to be the only mindful, compassionate agents for social change, nor can we even expect that they will take up that role. We must change our perceptions, beginning with the acceptance that we are all members of the same tribe and must take our membership seriously.

Once we have achieved a Global Mind, we will remember the damage we have done. This will be difficult and painful, but self-reflection is an important component to the Global Mind concept. Reflection reveals lessons and choices. Do we keep repeating the cultural patterns of competition and domination? Or do we invent a new way to be human starting now in the 21st century?

Without a shared humanistic purpose, we will simply repeat the patterns that promote an "us versus them" narrative until we are extinct.

Focusing on the creation of Global Mind must become a priority—one brain/mind at a time, one tweet at a time, and one conversation at a time, until the discourse is a habit and a social movement.

Edited by Nisha Kulkarni

nisha@nishakkulkarni.com

— Published on February 5, 2020

Chapter 9
The We-Team

Co-parenting after Divorce in the Age of COVID

Marriage is one of the casualties of the COVID pandemic. To help families navigate this massive addition to the stress load, I make use of the power of language.

The 'We-team' is a mindful practice for couples to create trust beyond divorce, beyond the conflicts of 'my story' against 'your story.' The We-team is a safe place for ex-partners and their children. The experience of 'We' respects 'me' and 'you.' Marriages that fail to create We-team experiences will suffer from chronic conflict. If they divorce in anger, the children will grow up in an emotional danger zone between them.

In my 30 years of helping families navigate toxic stress, I find that most parents can put their children's well-being before their own. A willingness to create a post-divorce We-team as co-parents are critical to preventing toxic stress that derails child development. After divorce, cultivating a co-parenting 'We-team' experience is imperative.

Co-parent We-teams remain calm and connected. They practice staying in the co-parent conversation and mindfully navigate away from toxic marital stress triggers. They do not blame one another. Their focus is on their children. They respect and accept that their parenting styles are different. This plays a critical role in helping families retain good parenting, no matter what their personal stresses might be.

Individuals in a couple live in several narratives simultaneously: partner, parent, individual, adult child, etc. Divorce can rupture all these attachments and do serious damage to the developing children in the family system. A resentful spouse can become an angry, distracted parent. A self-pitying divorcee can withdraw from parenting. Contempt between couples contaminates co-parenting in the eyes of children triggering toxic stress.

With the divorce rate soaring, the toll on children is profound and life-altering. We know that divorce, itself, does not have long term detriments on child development if it is managed by calm parents. But many divorcing couples live in the chronic, toxic stress of resentment and self-pity long after the divorce is settled. It is the toxic stress and the loss of parenting that does damage to the developing brain/mind of children.

We-team Benefits

In healthy couples and families, 'we' experiences create trust, inspire creativity, foster strong identities, and empower emotional resilience to the adversities of life. The brain's stress regulatory system needs consistency in early life to develop a secure attachment to oneself and others. Every child wants to have we-time with each parent. Positive bonds grow when parents emotionally attune with their child. Attuned parents bring attention to their children, show empathy for their struggles, and validate their efforts to master their developmental hurdles.

We-teams allow emotional communication to flow back and forth in families. A deep sense of intimacy and trust emerges, and it can last a lifetime. A secure We-team develops the skills to process the natural negative emotions triggered by disappointments in expectations. Disconnecting emotionally is normal. Reconnecting requires skill.

Making time for regular We-team meetings to process negative emotions is critical to a resilient co-parent bond. Divorced couples often do not have these skills. To protect the children from post-divorce stress, couples need to practice We-team mindfulness for co-parenting.

We-team meetings allow each partner to express their feelings of fear, anger, and confusion without blaming anyone. Owning one's feelings and sharing them cultivates empathy and trust between divorced parents. In a turn-taking conversation, without interruption, co-parents can jointly focus on diffusing stress to protect their children. The conversation also allows for requests and commitments to be heard. In an early divorce, it is helpful to structure regular meetings to prevent acute stress from becoming long-lasting and toxic.

I always remind young couples to cultivate true friendship, accepting each other as unique and different. When disappointments occur, blaming is commonly triggered. Practicing acceptance of these painful disconnections and sharing the feelings without blame recovers the brain/mind link and activates empathy and gratitude in the partnership.

We-team experience and memories are the foundation of true friendship. Long-lasting marital satisfaction is reflected in couples that describe each other as "my best friend." Friendship, not romance, is the key to longevity, happiness, and healthy children.

— Published on February 13, 2020

Chapter 10
Beyond Global Burnout

Cultural Evolution Imperative
Promoting Mindful Change

We live in a world that is continuously changing at an ever-increasing rate. Our creative nature drives us to explore and invent —'make it new; make it better'. We are also emotionally reacting to the changes we make—excitement about our inventiveness, inspiration to make newer things, obsession with applying our creativity to make life easier, and compulsion to pursue the next version of the things we make.

And we live in perpetual conflict between our wish to change and our fear of change. What happens if we lose our privacy? What happens if robotics takes our jobs? What happens if…? The worry about tomorrow paralyzes our actions in the present to solve and prevent catastrophic events.

We are facing world-changing processes that escalate this conflict to a level of global burnout.

The existential conflicts are well known. They are the 'what is' in the present: the ecosystem, our political rivalries, religious beliefs, technology, and much more. But the list does not include us, the creators of these conflicts. We have yet to put ourselves on the list of what must change if we are to adapt to the new world we have created.

We must change. We must take an inventory of our own self-sabotaging nature. We must evaluate our selfish behaviors and attitudes to see how they contribute to our own demise. We must confront our perpetual denial, rationalizing, and minimizing the damage we do to ourselves as a species and to the planet. We must be accountable to ourselves.

I recently listened to a talk by Halla Tomasdottir, CEO of Plan B. Their mission statement states:

"We're working to redefine the culture of accountability in business, for our companies, communities and future generations, by creating and cascading new norms of corporate leadership that can build a better world."

The boundless possibilities of human creativity await implementation. We have the technology to generate a mindful, global culture that respects all human life as sacred. Our science provides a fledgling understanding of how our brain works. We know that our basic sciences can be translated into social policy and new cultural values. We can affect climate change, air and water pollution, economic disparity, and world hunger. We can put an end to the constant flow of refugees by reframing our concept of what it means to be human.

Our ingenuity to make these applications from science to culture lies in the minds of our children. But our children need parents. Mindful parenting in this generation is critical to guide, to inspire, and to encourage our children to take the risks necessary to promote a mindful culture for themselves and future generations.

Mindful Families and Generation Delta

The next generation, call them 'generation delta' (delta is the symbol for change in mathematics), holds the potential for mindful cultural evolution. A mindful human family, one that sees itself as a critical part of the whole of our species, is the crucible for cultural evolution. When mindfulness shapes the family values that nourish children, the hope for a successful cultural transformation is possible.

Greta Thunberg exemplifies mindfulness, courage, and determination to enact a global mind. Her actions are based on facts and fact-based theories, and she speaks truth to power, that rare trait that kindles change through inspiration. She started a wave of global awareness that holds the potential for change if the present adults in power validate her call to action. We shall see.

Beyond Global Burnout

Imagine a world where the screen/brain interface is built-in and connects us to each other with positive emotion. Information flows for creativity, for solving the existential threats of climate change. Human connectivity regulates the charged competition that thrives on corruption in a political zero-sum game. Financial systems are transparent and economic disparity reduces, providing financial security across socioeconomic strata.

This is not a utopian fantasy. This is a possibility. The key to unlocking the human potential to evolve is vastly expanding mindfulness practices. When billions of human brains attain greater emotional self-regulation, empowering their innate compassion, a global "we-team" can emerge. Evolving our global village into a mindful community is a possibility and a necessity if we are to attain dynamic equilibrium for our biosphere.

The time is now to begin personal mindful practices, to charge social media with positive emotions. We must explore new ways to generate self-awareness and compassion for all. Educating our children in mindfulness and emotional intelligence is critical to strengthen the fabric of families.

It may take a generation before the heads of business and the government can reframe 'growth' as a human character factor rather than financial greed. Sustainability, not financial profit, must become the essence of successful businesses.

Evolving our world beyond the threat of global burnout is a possible reality. It begins with one brain at a time, practicing the boundless explorations of each mind and one family at a time, nourishing mindful attitudes and behaviors in the children. When mindfulness is a global phenomenon, we may enter a new epoch of human history.

edited by Nisha Kulkarni nishakkulkarni.com

— Published on February 18, 2020

PART II
COVID STRESS

Chapter 11
The Creativity Machine and Global Burnout

The Mindful Creativity Imperative

We are blessed with a brain—a creativity machine—that is a master of survival. But creativity has a dark side, and its by-products can be self-destructive. We have been so successful in colonizing every corner of the planet that our waste products are contaminating its viability. We must address the toxic consequences of our success—our problems spring from our own self-sabotaging attitudes and behaviors. It is imperative that we become more mindfully aware of balancing our creative impulses with a sustainable environment.

Andy Warhol

One of the most creative minds of the 20th century was artist Andy Warhol. His personal experiences using art to help him overcome severe stress, from childhood illness to surviving an assassination attempt, exemplifies how creativity can support survival. My relationship with Warhol can best be described as a 10-year-long conversation that started in 1976—at the opening for his print series, *Ladies and Gentlemen*—up until Christmas 1986, when he agreed to do an interview for my book, *The Art Imperative: The Secret Power of Art.*

As I think about creativity, global burnout, and Global Mind, I do wonder what Warhol would say about the world today.

Of one thing I am sure: had he lived Warhol would be talking about global burnout. He was, as they say, "ahead of his time": Warhol made computer-generated art before personal computers were the norm; his constant flow of gossip was an early form of personal branding and social media; and he even commissioned his own robot.

If his work is any indication, Warhol would have continued to be a nonstop source of creativity, unafraid to spotlight our world on the existential brink. He was already interested in issues that are so current: impermanence with his painting "Skulls"; 102 abstract canvases that provoke self-reflection with "Shadows"; and handgun violence with his "Guns." Undoubtedly, he would have challenged us to look at our roles in the world—especially at our current pop cultural icons—and how we are responsible for the damage done as much as the mindful healing we can inspire.

Warhol observed,

> *"Human beings are born solitary, but everywhere they are in chains—daisy chains—of interactivity. Social actions are makeshift forms, often courageous, sometimes ridiculous, always strange. And in a way, every social action is a negotiation, a*

compromise between 'his,' 'her,' or 'their' wish and yours."

Mindful Creativity

Warhol is just one example of how reflection is at the core of creativity. We are all creative and therefore all possess the capacity for mindful reflection. But we need a more *mindful* creativity.

We have paid little attention to how our creative advances have caused worldwide conflict and destruction. Our internet is unregulated, hijacked by greed, and—like with tobacco usage in the 20th century—its toxic effects are minimized. We did not calculate the toxic effects of carbon fuel on our biosphere. The human burnout rate in overcrowded cities is soaring. We are not able to deliver food to starving nations. And our medicines are creating mutations that threaten pandemic disease.

Our creativity may have tapped into our self-sabotaging attitudes and behaviors, but it has also promoted greater mindfulness and community. We achieved abstract beauty in the cave paintings 40,000 years ago. We invented scientific objectivity at the dawn of civilization. We created agricultural and trade systems that can feed people in different parts of the world. We have transportation systems that make the world more of an accessible village. We built cities that support tens of millions of people. We discovered vaccinations that eradicate widespread disease. We have created a global emotional brain—the internet—that connects everyone with just a smartphone. Our innate compassion has evolved diverse global cultures.

Our mindful creativity has no limit and can be a force for positive change.

Creating Changes Within Ourselves

Warhol's words address this creative challenge for us all:

"When people are ready to, they change. They never do it before then, and sometimes they

die before they get around to it. You can't make them change if they don't want to, just like when they do want to, you can't stop them."

We must focus on our individual creative potential, which can only contribute to the collective whole. And, to take a page from Warhol's book, today's pop culture can empower collective evolution toward species tribalism by encouraging creativity, self-reflection, and collaboration on a shared "we" narrative.

Edited by Nisha Kulkarni
nisha@nishakkulkarni.com
— Published on February 25, 2020

Chapter 12
Global Mind Against Pandemic

The Creativity Imperative

Creativity in Crisis

Coronavirus (COVID-19) is triggering a stress reaction in our brains. With mindful practice, we can accept the fact of the pandemic and activate a profound creative response to mobilize creative resilience. Every time we find our mind distracted by a 'what if' thought about the virus, we can refocus our attention to our body, breathe deeply a few times, and focus on gratitude for our body, our mind, and those we love.

Mindful practice empowers us to face crisis. In crisis, the brain literally freezes. It stops doing. As cognitive and emotional circuits boot up to process the threatening event horizon of the moment, it reflects on the situation rather than fight or flee. It is in this glimpse of imagined outcomes that the mind draws on experience, opens awareness to inventive solutions, and makes critical decisions to act. This is the moment where mind directs the body to calm down, to activate creative mindfulness, and to experiment with life-saving action. This process, our genetic heritage, has protected *homo sapiens* for millennia.

If we use this crisis in human history as a mirror of our behavior, we can begin to resolve the natural conflict between our self-centered attitudes and behaviors and our collective creativity.

Crisis recruits our primordial tribal instincts to band together for survival against a common enemy. Collective creativity, grounded in science, objectivity, and compassion lights the way toward a leap in cultural evolution that may finally empower *Species Tribalism*—we are all brothers and sisters.

We are participating in transforming human history. It is time to rethink the global village. It is time to redesign our relationships with every human being for the survival of our species. It is time to mobilize cultural evolution.

Coronavirus = *Species Tribalism.*

Beyond Crisis Toward Global Humanism

COVID-19 triggers our deepest fears. The virus is also activating our greatest potential—the hardwired ability to calm down in the face of crisis, to connect mindfully with each other, and to create solutions to the problem.

Our global community is an emergency room. Life as we know it has stopped. Every family is threatened. Our doctors and nurses are risking their lives as warriors at the front line of this new battle. The basic sciences are in full-on search for new tools to protect our species.

It is a time for collective creativity. A human imperative drives cooperation and coordination with each other to protect the global village. We are seeing an awakening to the stark fact that our attitudes and behaviors can be the difference between life and death.

Our brains are loading new memories. Powerful traumatic images of our collapsing world order are being tattooed into our brains. The acute stress we are enduring as the pandemic leaps across borders, as the death tolls rise, will give way to massive post-traumatic stress that will shape our future. We will be faced with questions and choices of how we adapt.

Nature demands a creative response if we are to evolve from the world we knew. Our survival requires a collective action. Preventing the spread of disease requires that we reflect on our traditions, prejudices, and nationalistic interests if our species is to survive.

The socioeconomic structures that create financial disparity in the world are collapsing. We have a robust capacity to create jobs and prosperity and to design a new world and create a sustainable biosphere. But the distribution of financial security is skewed. Biology is challenging our financial institutions.

Medical science is playing a critical role in shaping the new world. Humanism, the core of medical practice, is acquiring new status in policy and action. Medical intelligence is the new foundation of national and global security. Global warming, terrorism, and gender politics are being preempted. Military force is being retooled to fight a microscopic enemy. Political interests will be driven by life and death decisions. Religious dogma is challenged by humane, spiritual meaning.

Choosing Creative Optimism

As individuals, we can find balance in riding through the crisis. Like surfers on a wave—

balancing our mind (the surfer) and body (the surfboard) on the event horizon of the COVID-19 (the wave)—must be mindfully present to the moment. Our stress system can be easily distracted and trigger a 'wipe-out'.

As surfers say, 'The wave is a great teacher of mindfulness'. We can use COVID-19 as an experiment in human creativity, cultivating our genetic potential as the foundation of a new epoch of *Species Tribalism*.

We have been through this before. After the Bubonic Plague annihilated 75 to 200 million people (30-60% of Europe), we created the Renaissance.

— Published on March 23, 2020

Chapter 13
Creativity Versus Pandemic

Your Brain is a Creativity Machine
The Covid-19 Pandemic is triggering more worried brains than we have ever seen. We are in crisis. It is a time for each of us to learn and practice some very simple mindfulness practices to prevent our own burnout.

Activating our inborn creative resilience will empower us to navigate the wave of the virus and regulate our brain's stress response. Our mind can turn off the body's freeze-fight-flight response and activate the brain/mind's calm-connect-creativity power.

This is the beginning of a new, creative era in human history where we can literally evolve long-term changes in our global village—*species tribalism.*

The Creativity Machine and Resilience

Our brains are creativity machines built to adapt in new ways for survival. We can activate the creativity brain state with some simple practices—daydreaming and meditation. With mindful effort we can refocus our attention from stress-driven 'doing' (convergent brain-state) to mindfully calm 'being' (divergent brain-state). Learning to take time to 'be' in a daydream is a natural antidote to stress.

In this divergent brain state, attention is turned inward. Many neural networks communicate with each other, like a town hall meeting where feelings, perceptions, memories, and imagery are synchronized. The imagination and problem-solving spring from this brain state. Many of us experience this while taking a shower or watching the river flow. Isaac Newton's discovery of gravity is an example of scientific creativity emerging while daydreaming.

Personal Creativity

Creativity is a private, personal experience. It is often non-conscious. Creative experiences can lead to new ideas and behaviors. If we cultivate and respect the power of creativity as a natural antidote to stress, we benefit in numerous ways.

Being mindfully present when we do everyday things like brushing your teeth, or cooking opens the mind to novelty and serious fun. The daydreaming brain can refresh our 'stuck' problem solving abilities and reboot our perspective.

Social Distancing and Quarantine

We are all spending time indoors. It is the perfect opportunity to reframe the feelings of being prisoner. We can choose to create this time as a retreat into ourselves. Given the deadly consequences that may occur to those we know, it is a time for spiritual reflection. Gratitude for life, for our body, our mind, and those we love deepens our ability to enjoy one day at a time. During reflections, the creative brain empowers our mind's story of personal meaning. A deepening respect for our lives can motivate changes in attitudes and behaviors.

Nature's Great Teaching

Nature provides us with life, consciousness, and love. She is a great teacher. The novel coronavirus, a natural life-form struggling to survive, brings a great teaching to us all—the fact of impermanence. When our mortality is so dramatically present, fragile, and palpable, we can awake to the sacred gift of life. Sharing the gift with others opens our minds to relax in the fact of our impermanence and cherish each breath. The great gift of consciousness is that we can enjoy being alive, no matter how long we have.

Connecting and Amplifying Meaning

We have an opportunity to improve our tech skills in connecting with each other creatively. We may evolve from self-centered chatter, and meaningless social media, to more compassionate communication. Inspiring each other with positive experiences can make your day.

As a city dweller, I rarely hear birdsong. My sister sent me a video from rural Texas so I could watch a herd of cows grazing and listen to them chewing to a chorus of sparrows chattering—it made my day!

— Published on March 30, 2020

Chapter 14
Dance with Pandemic

From the Black Plague to Coronavirus

As physicians, we are trained to face death with compassion, to support nature's built-in resilience to disease, and to understand the laws of the life/death cycle to ease human suffering. The physician works at the tipping point between life and death, combining the best of science and art. In its deepest core, the practice of medicine aims to promote human vitality for meaningful action during the body's lifespan. The sacred jewel of consciousness found in every human body is its creative mind.

Our brain is a creativity machine. Our mindful awareness and reflective consciousness generate meaningful narratives that amplify our tribal nature to form groups for optimizing survival. When our individual brain/mind forms secure bonds with others, we generate awesome creative resilience. As a species, we can go beyond the science and art of medicine by applying the fundamentals of individual resilience to human cultural evolution. Developing 'species tribalism' is the implicit goal for human organizations. As we use technology to activate global mindfulness, we may discover that our misperception of the 'war with coronavirus' is better framed as a 'dance with death'.

Like the artists Guyot Marchant and Hans Holbein of the post Bubonic plague era in medieval times, we need to reframe our relationship with nature and impermanence to inspire human creativity. Human creative resilience to the millions of deaths during the black plague produced an art form called the 'dance macabre,' where skeletons led the procession of people from the Pope to Kings to paupers parading to the grave. The profundity of these images helped people face the fear of death. By reframing our natural fear of death toward acceptance of impermanence, we can empower our creativity. Joy in life, wonderment at awareness, and embracing our deep emotional connectivity spawned the Renaissance—literally advancing human culture toward a fearless creative drive that would touch all human beings.

COVID-19 challenges our species to reflect on our greed and arrogance in respect to nature. Our reckless consumption of natural resources has pushed the biosphere to an existential brink. Our compulsion to kill each other in mindless wars knows no end. Death is as much a product of human behavior as it is a natural occurrence. The mindless attitudes of greed and arrogance perpetuate human self-sabotage.

By reframing our relationship with nature and the life/death cycle in the face of COVID-19, we may realize that understanding resilience to this virus requires that we activate our full potential to calm down, to connect with each other as a species, and to create a new global culture based on compassion and wisdom. The power of science and art can overcome the compulsion for greed and arrogance. Cultivating trust between all human beings is a great leap for mankind. By using our brilliant tools from Artificial Intelligence to social media, we may generate a 'global mind' from the global brain of the internet. As we evolve a mindful humanist culture that focuses of sustainability for ourselves on this planet, we hold the potential for using COVID-19 as an inspiration for new life, rather than seeing it as a specter of death.

Danse Macabre by Hans Holbein

— Published on May 14, 2020

Chapter 15
COVID Stress: What Is! Vs. What If?

Facts Against Fears
First Lessons in Facing Crisis

During my first per-med year in college, I worked 60 hours a week as a firefighter in Port Arthur, Texas. My brain was tattooed with the smell of a burning oil refinery fire—Port Arthur being the second largest oil refinery site in the world. It took fifty fire trucks two days to dampen a potential disaster after a giant oil container exploded killing three men. Spending 12 hours sitting on a firehose 30-yards from a red-hot oil tank left a post-traumatic olfactory memory in my brain.

In those twelve hours, I had a singular intrusive thought: *What if?* What if the steel tank gave way? What if a million gallons of burning oil washed over us? What if my life ended at age 19?

The raging fire billowed smoke thousands of feet into the air. It could be seen for miles. What if this is my end? The self-centered, intrusive thought of *What if?* Burned in my brain like the raging fire.

The fear of dying was gradually extinguished by the camaraderie with 250 fellow firefighters during the long hours of toxic fumes and burning heat. By risking our lives together as a team, my attention was repeatedly refocused to coordinate action with my partner on managing a 2.5-inch diameter hose. Working with other firefighters to cool the blazing oil tank and mitigate disaster helped cool my brain, training me to accept *What Is!*

COVID STRESS: What IS! Against What IF?

Today, we are experiencing a global fire, the COVID-19 pandemic. Our brains are spontaneously hijacked by *What if?* What if my family dies? What if it can't be controlled? What if it destroys our economy?

It is time to challenge our brains fear response with Facts. We can extinguish the fears of *What if?* by thinking with mindful attention to facts, to *What is!* The fact is that the COVID fire will burn endlessly unless we stop it. We must work together to prevent a disaster. We must become a single army facing a ferocious, unpredictable enemy. Like firefighters, we need to prevent COVID from spreading. We must prevent a disaster that could wipe out millions of people. We have a shared mission—work together and save lives!

We have scientific expertise. We know how to mitigate the spread. We will develop treatments and perhaps a vaccine. We can prevent deaths if we work as a singular army, cooperating with clear guidelines. We can overcome our fears together.

The enemy is not the virus—the enemy is our fear.

When the brain is perpetually triggered by *what-if thinking* we generate toxic stress. Our attention is distracted from the present to a catastrophic future. And after weeks of this new reality, stress hormones build up—we suffer with toxic COVID stress. Perpetual *what-if thinking* can lead to anxiety, panic, and depression. We can feel like hostages.

The antidote to *what if thinking* is to focus our attention to *What IS!* Reframing our attention from tomorrow to today is precisely what is needed to face the fear of global death spiraling out of control. By living in the moment, paying attention to our body, regulating our breathing, we can cultivate gratitude for the miracle of life and self-awareness. This mindful reframing to *What Is* turns off the stress response, activating the *relaxation response.* By calming ourselves down and connecting with each other, we can participate in the critical mission of mitigating behaviors. It is in our love of life, our respect for each other, that we can collaborate to meet the challenge of Pandemic.

My first lessons in the sacredness of life were learned as a firefighter. We must face the COVID fire together willing to change our behaviors to protect others. At age 19, I became aware of the meaning of shared efforts to work together for survival. It is our deepest instinct as mammals to calm down, connect with each other, and fight the threat to our existence.

Many among us still live-in denial of the morbidity of this pandemic. Minimizing the deadly threat is widespread, even among public leaders. The counter-phobic response of disregarding proven mitigating behaviors or social distancing and masks reveals human self-sabotaging arrogance at its worst.

It takes extra effort to mindfully challenge our selfish urges to survive as individuals or fighting for ourselves. We must surrender to the fact that we are stronger together. Our global connectivity is the critical ingredient to overcoming this pandemic.

Our greatest survival instincts inspire us to calm down, connect with each other, and create new solutions for ourselves and our planet.

— Published on June 1, 2020

Chapter 16
Falling into COVID

The Fire and the Phoenix: A Personal Story in the Age of Pandemic

The first sunny Sunday in April invited me to venture out for a walk after isolating in place for a month of COVID retreat. Still a bit wobbly from multiple hip replacement surgeries, I put on my mask and gloves, picked up my trusty Brigg cane-handle umbrella that served as a support for stairs, and ventured back into the world. It was only six steps down my stoop to the stone walkway that led to the sidewalk. In the final step, as I looked up toward the street, my left heel caught onto the edge of the step, and I went sailing into the air. Weightless, falling, and startled, I reached to grab the railing to break my fall.

After what felt like an eternal second, my body smashed into the slate tiles, stopping my fall.

One breath, then two…I slowly recovered my awareness of what had happened. My mind scanned my body, hoping to feel the energy and the power to stand up. I could not move. The pain vibrated through every screaming cell of my being. I slowly reached into my jacket pocket, found my mobile phone, and called for help.

As I rode the ambulance to the emergency room, I asked myself, "How did that happen?" I had taken such care to step out into the COVID world.

After surgery—I had a steel rod implanted in my fractured tibia (my left lower leg)—I would have a week of hospitalization, in the time of pandemic, terrified that I would come home with COVID. The pain was severe for days. I had plenty of time for mindful reflection, remembering my life story, daydreaming. Searching for inspiration to push through the pain to do the physical therapy, I recalled my paternal grandfather, Felipe Romero, a

Mexican refugee from the revolution of 1910-20. He was a chef and a baker. His restaurant in Edinburgh, Texas burned to the ground. He took a job working as a cook in a prison to save money to build a bakery, his true passion. He called it El Fenix, after the mythical bird that is reborn by fire. Although he died before I could meet him, his name and his story have been a life-long muse for my creative resilience during adversity across my life.

Activating my brain's creativity reframed my fear, mitigated my pain, and inspired me to recover my mind-body link. Finding a personal story of inspiration to recreate oneself with new vigor is the key to resilience.

As I re-remembered every moment before the fall, I realized that my body was very frightened about going out. Despite my medical training, my years of mindfulness practice, and a career of helping people face their fears, I did not shepherd my body gently down the stairs. Instead, my ego courageously charged into the outing with a manly stride and tripped over my own feet.

What a perfect metaphor for mindless, self-sabotaging arrogance.

My body was broken.

My inattention to my emotional insecurity and physical frailty in the time of pandemic cost me dearly: pain, stress, exposure to high-risk environments.

I thank the miracle of my mind, with its natural acceptance of 'What Is'. 'What Is,' in each-and-every moment, is constantly changing. My mind instinctively focuses on my body's pain. With effortful attention, I can bring deep compassion to my body, as a parent would for a child. Activating mindful gratitude for my body strengthens this mysterious and miraculous coupling of mind-body existence.

Breaking my body, once again, enduring the surgical reconstruction, working through the rehabilitation, and relearning how to sit, to stand, to walk, was like being an infant, a toddler, and eventually feeling like an adult.

Falling into COVID was a glimpse into timelessness. My fear, my fall, and the pain of my broken body awakened a deep awareness of my precious physical being. I am impermanent, fragile, and resilient. With gratitude for each step my body takes, my mind's focus is fueled by each breath. I feel the joy of living as my mind-body link is welded back together by the fire of the Phoenix.

The Phoenix myth, thanks to my grandfather, kindled my creative resilience. By reframing the 'fire of COVID' as a spark of rebirth, I have activated my 'inner Phoenix,' empowering my endurance to rehabilitate the damage to my body. I have returned to the new world of telemedicine to help others navigate the greatest threat to global culture, individually and collectively.

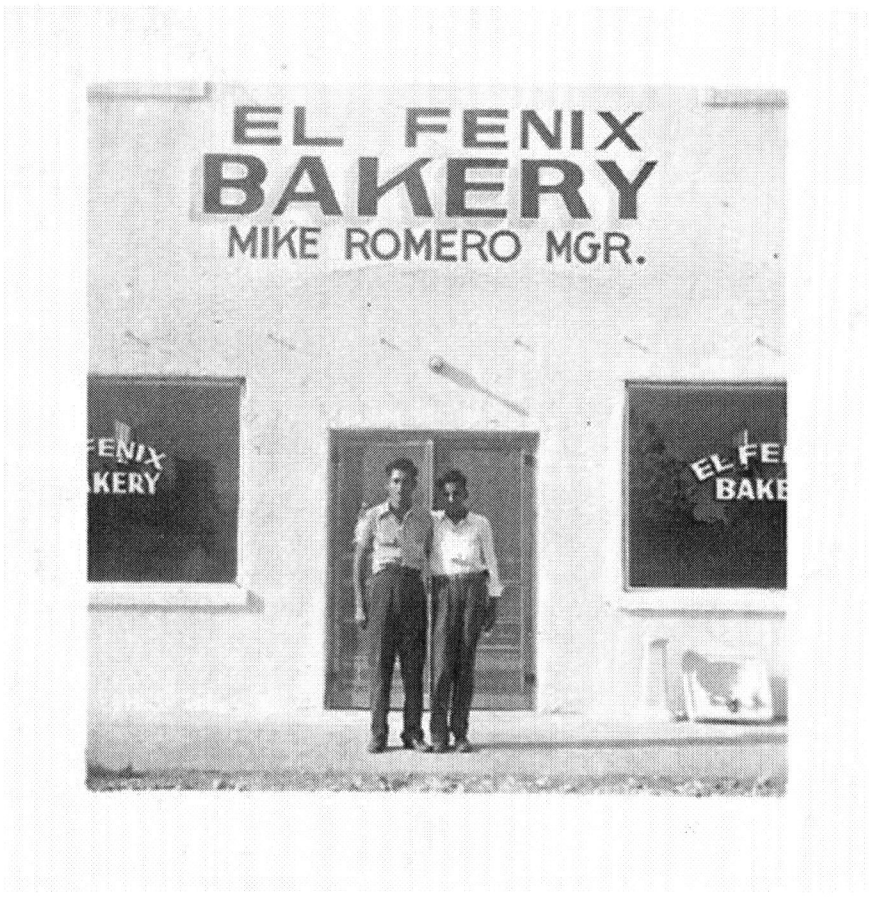

My Grandfather's Legacy

— Published on June 25, 2020

PART III
CREATIVE INTELLIGENCE =
SURVIVAL

Chapter 17
Creative Intelligence

The Post-Covid, Global Village Imperative
I had my first *Covax* jab (Covid vaccinations). My personal stress load plummeted, and my creativity got a booster shot. Lowered stress = increased creativity! I know there is *No Going Back* to the pre-covid world. We must reinvent ourselves and recreate the world. We must be mindful, practical, compassionate, and connected on a global level. We must redefine ourselves as a human family, a single race of *homo sapiens* (modern human beings). It is time to proactively empower the idea and practice of *Species Tribalism*. We must recruit and coordinate our individual and collective *Creative Intelligence* (CI). Resilience + Creativity = Creative Intelligence.

During this last year, the "Earth Stood Still." I closed my office and adapted my private practice in family psychiatry with telemedicine. I reframed the mandate for social distancing as a year-long, personal retreat for mindfulness practice, daydreaming and creative problem solving. I was inspired by Ariana Huffington's platform, thriveglobal.com, and her mission is to *"go beyond raising awareness and create something real and tangible that would help individuals, companies and communities improve their well-being and performance and unlock their greatest potential."*

I wrote fifteen essays for Thrive Global. In Chapter 16, "Falling into Covid," I reflected about breaking my leg on my first post-lockdown stroll. We can all feel like victims and hostages, especially with two surgeries and prolonged rehabilitation. Practicing mindful meditation and with my program, 6Rs for *Creative Intelligence*, I transformed the negative stress into creativity.

From Logosoma Brain Training to Creative Intelligence

In the last decade of clinical practice, I developed *Logosoma Brain Training* (1986), method for relationship stress management, into a fresh concept: *6Rs for Creative Intelligence* training. Advances in the neuroscience of creativity inspired my personal creativity to integrate my fifty years of practice in Tibetan and Zen meditation, my lifelong experiences as an artist (painting, photography, filmmaking), and techniques from Tibetan dream yoga.

By integrating multiple attentional practices, I developed the 6Rs for Creative Intelligence (CI). CI training activates the brain's neuroplasticity. The brain is a creativity machine that can rewire itself. We can continue learning throughout life. The neural networks of our sense-of-self can be changed by unlearning old patterns and learning new attitudes, behaviors, and values.

The 6Rs for Creative Intelligence recruit the brain's natural *default network* for creativity. By practicing these six steps, we activate a complex process of rewiring the neural networks of our sense-of-self. We can also approach reinventing global culture to face the existential challenges that face our species. The process holds the potential for amplifying individual and collective Creative Intelligence.

(1) By *Remembering* negative emotional experiences (especially pandemic memories), we can activate our cognitive ability to

(2) *Reflect* on our perception of ourselves as victims or hostages. Using our ability to

(3) *Reframe* our experiences, we can practice acceptance of the pain of living with gratitude for our creativity. Using our imagination, we can

(4) *Reimagine* reality. In creative conversations we can

(5) *Reinvent* ways of living. We must create many new "blueprints" for living with each other, from the nuclear family to the ever-shrinking global village. Creating new "maps for cultural change" guide

(6) *Reconnecting* global village communication in all areas of human endeavor.

To prevent future global catastrophes, it is imperative to focus our individual and collective Creative Intelligence to meet the existential threats we face. Unless we band together in a narrative of species tribalism, the challenges of climate change and future pandemic, world hunger, mass migrations, and socioeconomic disparity can produce global systemic burnout beyond imagination. Creative Intelligence training empowers personal creativity, and it empowers the collective social application toward cultural evolution—species tribalism.

— Published on March 8, 2021

Chapter 18
Nature's Challenge / Nature's Gift

Redefining Wellness for Survival

Nature's Challenge: *Survival*

Since the dawn of humankind, we have observed the cycles of nature and struggled to survive in these powerful patterns. Life and death, night and day, the seasons, the ebb and flow of the tides, the arcs of the sun and moon, inspire human beings to "make sense" of these phenomena with explanatory narratives. In our relationships to each other, these cyclic patterns show up as love and fear, trust and mistrust, creative collaboration, and destructive adversity. We live in these cyclic patterns, moment by moment. We can accept them and adapt to them creatively, or we can challenge them and attempt to control them. These patterns of conflict inform much of human history. Nature's Challenge: *The Dance of Death*

The COVID pandemic presents another of Nature's challenges to humankind. Add it to the global list of climate change, mass migrations, socioeconomic disparity, and political instability. Species survival has never experienced such complexity on a worldwide scale. Human Creative Intelligence, the innate creative response to adversity that mobilizes the coordination of group action and cooperation, is facing rapidly escalating challenges from nature.

Life against death is perpetual. Humankind is struggling to recover our biopsychosocial balance with the biosphere. The ancient zero-sum game of "man against nature" has misguided our application of science, technology, commerce, and religious beliefs into a self-sabotaging pattern of repetitious creativity and destructivity. COVID has revealed vast cultural differences in mortality based on racial and socioeconomic demographics.

We still create cultural systems from the perception of infantile reality: *me against you, winner take all*. We have yet to create cultural system from the kindergarten curriculum: *take turns and share*. Greed drives socioeconomic and military-industrial systems. Wealth and power hold the world hostage to the will of a small percentage of people. Human values remain a minority in the face of the compulsive quest for corporate and national dominance.

Generating a *Global Mind* from the Global Brain

Our invention of the internet empowers the potential to generate a *Global Mind* from the *Global Brain* of the internet. The evolution of a self-regulating *Global Mind* is inevitable. Will it be charged with humanistic values, reciprocal trust, and empathy? Or will it simply extend the 10,000-year-old structure of master-subject culture that has permeated human history. Currently the internet is being used as a self-centered stimulant, largely mindless, to trigger adrenalin driven excitement that drives behaviors to enrich the owners of the system. The hamster-wheel patterns of repetitious, compulsive, greed-driven behaviors persist.

The only potential for self-parenting is our inborn individual Creative Intelligence. Using the skills for reflective cognition, we can empower creativity to rewire the neural networks of our brain that can collectively change patterns of civilization.

Nature's Gift: *COVID Time and Creative Intelligence Practice*

The paradox of surviving a pandemic requires both isolation and cooperation. The implicit "gift" from COVID is the *time* mandated for isolation and social distancing. Using the gift of time for contemplation, meditation, and reinventing ourselves in relation to others empowers resilience to the adversity of isolation. It is natural to suffer from stress and pain with separation and loss of loved ones, triggering cascades of toxic hormones that cause mental and emotional illnesses and self-sabotaging behaviors. The consequence is a post-covid wave of mental and emotional disorders. Depression, anxiety, addiction, family violence, obesity, and many other serious illnesses. Chronic stress hijacks the brain, leaving it without mindful or social self-regulation. The emotions of stress, anger, fear, and confusion, drive behaviors. The result is chaos, violence, and crime.

Creative Intelligence and Wellness

Redefining *Wellness* is critical to our survival. Wellness springs from the practice of Creative Intelligence, a creative approach to the practice of living. Wellness is kindled in mindful awareness of the present moment. One's perception of reality, whether it is painful or pleasurable, is relative to the individual's perception and experience. From the mundane experiences of hygiene, nutrition, sleeping, and exercise, our personal wellness forms the foundation of our resilience to stress and our joy in creating meaningful lives and relationships.

Wellness flourishes when we access our inborn *Creative Intelligence*. Nature has endowed us with biological resilience to adversity and an innate narrative for Creativity—the resilient *body* and the creative *story*. Creative Intelligence emerges with mindful integration of Nature's gifts: *Resilience + Creativity = Creative Intelligence*.

Sustaining Wellness through the pandemic is a biopsychosocial communication process that mitigates the natural stress reaction to the threat of chaos and death. Contemplation, cooperation, and the coordination of action are critical to this process of stress regulation.

The COVID pandemic stress load on individuals, families, and the economy has yet to be fully evaluated. Far beyond the death toll, chronic, toxic stress is triggering a tidal wave of mental and emotional damage. Human Creative Intelligence is challenged to develop Wellness Training for the species on a global level. Wellness practices mitigate stress and promote creativity and resilience. Cooperation in all fields of knowledge from science, the arts, economics, spiritual practices, sports, politics, must lead the way in placing *Wellness as the most important asset for species survival.*

Impermanence and Relativity: *Ancient Wisdom, Modern Science*

Like a physician for the human condition, Buddha's Four Noble Truth's defined *Impermanence* as the core of all human suffering. Fear of the loss of our attachments to our body, our families, our possessions triggers stress. Chronic stress is toxic to the body, the mind, and society.

The COVID pandemic reminds us of our impermanence. Nature's challenge to our species with extinction level threats, from comets to Covid, recruits our Creative Intelligence for new survival strategies. Buddha identified our conscious awareness as the core of our perception of reality. Like Einstein, he identified "reality" as relative to the observer. If we train our mindful awareness to accept the *"truth" of impermanence and relativity*, we can enjoy our lives with gratitude in the present, even in the face of disaster. Neuroscience has demonstrated that mindful practices empower resilience to toxic, traumatic stress.

The Creative Brain: *Being and Doing* The brain has built in creative powers that emerge in childhood and can be cultivated throughout life. Cultivating the brain state for creativity is accomplished by the simple act of childlike daydreaming. The only requirement to activate Creative Intelligence is secure emotional attachments to others in a calm body and clear communication. The ability to practice this critical process begins in the family during childhood.

Humanistic Optimism: *Art, Science, and Species Tribalism Imperative*

Historically, science and art help people across cultures adapt. Both the arts and sciences are grounded in the brain states required for Creative Intelligence. To meet Nature's challenge, the universal acceptance of the arts and sciences holds the key to collective survival. Emotional self-regulation as a Species requires shared narratives of trust and respect. Science is dependent on peer review, not faith. Art communicates directly to conscious and non-conscious cognition and emotion. Art and science kindle wonder, activate the creative imagination, and bond people with different values. New information continually redefines action to successfully live and work together. Any social structure that empowers collective, global resilience will be grounded in

Creative Intelligence and manifest in science and promote art.

— Published on June 13, 2021

Chapter 19
Redefining Wellness

Creative Intelligence

Wellness and Creative Intelligence

Redefining Wellness is critical to our survival. By reframing wellness as a practice of awareness in action, not a state of being, we mobilize the mind-body connections to activate Creative Intelligence. "I do wellness practices" vs. "I am well." Wellness practices connect us socially, rather than isolate us in our own self-centered pursuits. By reinventing Wellness as a process, we empower social connectivity, versus self-centered, ego-driven attainment. We realize our genetic heritage is designed to expand the awareness of "Me" to the creation of "We."

Wellness flourishes when we access our inborn Creative Intelligence. Nature has endowed us with biological resilience to adversity and an innate narrative for Creativity—the resilient body and the creative story. Creative Intelligence emerges with mindful integration of Nature's gifts: Resilience + Creativity = Creative Intelligence.

Wellness is kindled in one's perception of reality, whether it is painful or pleasurable. The individual's perceptions and experiences are private.

We can cultivate a mindful attitude toward the body by imagining: 'mind is a loving parent' and the 'body is a child.' This image empowers a seamless integration of protective nurturing in the mind-body connection. From the mundane experiences of hygiene, nutrition, sleeping, and exercise, our personal wellness forms the foundation of our resilience to stress and our joy in creating meaningful lives and relationships.

Expanding the concept of Wellness is critical to meet the health crisis challenges in the Global

Village: climate change, mass migrations, mental, emotional, and behavioral burnout.

Mitigating Post-COVID Burnout

Sustaining Wellness through the pandemic is a biopsychosocial communication process that mitigates the natural stress reaction to the threat of chaos and death. Contemplation, cooperation, and the coordination of action are critical to this process of stress regulation.

The COVID pandemic stress load on individuals, families and the economy has yet to be fully evaluated. Far beyond the death toll, chronic, toxic stress is triggering a tidal wave of mental and emotional damage. Human Creative Intelligence is challenged to develop Wellness Training for the species on a global level.

Wellness practices are rooted in ancient and modern traditions: Yoga, Tai Chi, meditation, and many other practices. A consilient (unity of knowledge) approach to mind-body experience is emerging. Social neuroscience expands the importance of attachment theory in human relationships. Secure attachment in relationships is created by stress regulation. Wellness practices mitigate the natural formation of toxic relationship stress and promote creativity and resilience. Cooperation in all fields of knowledge from science, the arts, economics, spiritual practices, sports, politics, must lead the way in placing Wellness as the most important asset for species survival.

Cultivating Global Mind Wellness

The internet is the Global Brain for the Global Village. The evolution of the Global Mind will require a social evolutionary process. Wellness practices are critical to social communication between ordinary individuals and social institutions. The bottom-up and top-down communication system has been empowered by the internet. Influences now reverberate between individuals and large social systems, from government, corporations, religions, and secular groups.

Although this social evolution enterprise is challenged by deeply rooted patterns of adversity, bias, and opposition, there are large movements from all domains of knowledge that acknowledge a Global Mind Imperative. Linking these various efforts in Wellness practices can kindle reciprocal amplification of the evolutionary process.
Small groups of like-minded entrepreneurs play a key role in the bottom-up link to large organizations. By focusing a diverse approach to Wellness, thinking 'outside the box' is activated. Recruiting change in the top-down values of large social systems requires Creative Intelligence Training. This is critical to the success of any evolutionary process.

— Published on June 16, 2021

Chapter 20
American Fear Now

The Creative Intelligence Imperative
Things fall apart. (1921)
W. B. Yeats
Make something from nothing.
Andy Warhol

As a family psychiatrist, I apply the S. O. A. P. template (Subjective, Objective, Assessment, Plan) to making assessments and treatment plans with stressed-out families Family systems under chronic stress will exhibit emotional, behavioral, and self-sabotaging symptoms that threaten to unravel the family bonds that secure resilience.

Upscaling this approach to the social systems in America today, I offer these observations and recommendations.

SUBJECTIVE

American culture is hijacked by fear. Existential threats include the COVID pandemic, climate change, mass shootings, racial violence, political gridlock, socioeconomic disparity, opioid addiction, devastating job loss, and many others. Mental and emotional consequences are emerging in a cultural post-traumatic stress wave across the nation. Helplessness, hopelessness, despair, rage, and terror have taken the nation hostage.

OBJECTIVE

7.9 Billion brains populate our planet. Stress hormones are engulfing these brains in increasing numbers. The medical consequences are clear: *burnout syndrome* on a planetary scale. The "job of being a member of civil society" is breaking down.

American Fear drives mass shootings (over 600 in 2020 and 220 by May 2021). Politically instigated fear focused the January 6th Insurrection. Cultural insecurity re-empowers racial bias and hatred. Gender identity evolution intoxicates the brain/minds of gender binary adherents. Intolerance, disgust, and contempt for the emergence of gender biodiversity bleeds into ancient religious dogmas that rationalize godly murder, empowering terrorism.

Fear of losing secure attachments to people, places, beliefs, ideas, and things, hijacks rational brains into mindless frenzy. Fear kindles suffering. Fear fulminates as a pandemic of social chaos triggers mass psychosis.

ASSESSMENT

Biosphere burnout, pandemic, mass migrations, addiction, mindless political gridlock are symptoms, not causes, of systemic chaos and *Global Burnout.* Society is unwell. The structures that support this teetering socioeconomic pyramid, where a small percentage of people own most of the world's wealth, are unsustainable. It is not time for another revolution. We do not have time or material resources to recover from race riots, gender wars, destructive outrage, insurrections, or systemic collapse. We must pool our energies, guided by our innate Creative Intelligence, to meet Nature's challenges of climate change, socioeconomic disparity, and food shortages.

As mammals, we freeze, fight, and flee in the face of danger. Human beings feel confusion, anger, and fear. The colossal stress load on humanity hijacks every brain. Not since Hiroshima has such a collective fear of self-annihilation hijacked the human mind. The Global Village feels like a hostage to Nature. We are on the brink of catastrophic cultural collapse.

The great creative enterprise of human culture teeters at a tipping point of toxic stress. Each brain is equipped with innate resilience and the capacity for creative problem-solving. Resilience + Creativity = Creative Intelligence. We are a

Creative Intelligent species. Our history reflects our ability to create "something from nothing." We are the most powerful creativity machine in the known universe.

Human beings are challenged by nature to activate their gift of Creative Intelligence. We must learn how to use it. We must evolve a new definition of ourselves, reimagining our mission in this life, on this planet, if we are to overcome the escalating adversity pandemic.

PLAN

Activating Global Creative Intelligence

Creative Intelligence must be trained, practiced, and guided from individual empowerment to social network evolution.

Cultural Wellness can only emerge through redefining the human mission towards species survival—*Species Tribalism*. Social evolution will require of massive infusion of Creative

Intelligence: the inborn calm-connect-create response to stress. Every human brain is equipped for developing Creative Intelligence.

As the most advanced creativity machine in the universe, each human brain/mind can learn to regulate its own perceptions of stress. Simple practices based on gratitude and respect for human life, for consciousness, for fellowship, hold the potential to redefine how families teach children, how tribal groups view each other, how gender identities coordinate living together, and how different political models cooperate for the greater good.

Greed for wealth and power has been the driving force in human culture for 10,000 years. Perhaps the current extinction level threats may trigger social evolution, based on the Golden Rule of childhood and the kindergarten curriculum: "Take turns and share."

PROGNOSIS: *Guarded*

Will our self-sabotaging behaviors find a balance to navigate beyond this perfect storm of cultural demise?

Will our Creative Intelligence sublimate self-centered greed into greed for species survival giving birth to *Species Tribalism*?

It is up to us.

— Published on June 29, 2021

About the Author

Phillip E. Romero MD, **PHILLIP E. ROMERO, M.D. Family Psychiatrist, author, artist at PHILLIP E. ROMERO, M.D.**

Phillip Romero, MD, private practice in family psychiatry, retired Asst. Clinical Professor of Psychiatry, New York-Presbyterian Hospital-Weill Medical College, Cornell Univ., author of 'Phantom Stress: Brain Training to Master Relationship Stress (2010) and 'The Art Imperative, The Secret Power of Art' (2010), artist, filmmaker of CREATIVITY = SURVIVAL series.

Printed in Great Britain
by Amazon